sallow

Frances Presley

images by Irma Irsara

Open House Editions

Published by Open House Editions
an imprint of Leafe Press
www.leafepress.com

The text is copyright © Frances Presley, 2016. All rights reserved.

The images are copyright © Irma Irsara, 2016. All rights reserved.

ISBN 978-0-9574048-7-8

Acknowledgements

Poems have appeared in the following journals and I would like to thank the editors: *Long Poem Magazine*, Linda Black and Lucy Hamilton; *Poetry Wales*, Nia Davies

Some of these poems were part of a performance with Robert Minhinnick at SJ Fowler and Nia Davies' Enemies/ Gelynion event in Swansea in 2015.

I would also like to thank Harriet Tarlo for permission to publish her response to 'crack willow'.

sallow

FRANCES PRESLEY

images by IRMA IRSARA

willow

sunset in flood
                Red   across   the Levels

       paddy   fields

  import   java

               smooth watEr

              ~~WILLOW ENGLISH~~

           a   craft   sign
                         Dipping
            into water

each   tree   reflects

          black   branch

          over   branch

          un   folds

          Rorschach   blotch

          ink   sp   Read

crack willow

in dark unknown leaves
unidentified
without an app
non sun

      water plane falls
      in a mask

          bog   reeds
          plastic   flutes
          stem   champagne
            held   triumph
          dis   mantles

a series of masks
each flabbier
than the last

       under a m(ask)
       hold up
            YES or NO

                        not to answer
                        friend or unfriend

the north crawls sideways
              across the water
                        memoring slabs

       a pontoon
            out grown   out worn
                   some flaked skin
                          sorshed

                                    FP

not dark
not app
not mask

wet-silvery green over
      high brown-gold bracken
skirting, un-opening
      around us, us around
      and through
      water

         slabbing down sound

    where two discourse
        ways and where
fore, back
          which tree might serve
    us or refuse

      to be native, not native

   any assertion
     or naming

          migrated, she said, round
       stone and water, bridging gaping float

    right into the clough   sending wild, scrawny shoots

      up from rot-scent ground, and all its implications

                       HT

   contorting to whatever
angle   twist

                              branch split
                inside itself
                                        curve splinter

                        view through

                              clough held space

                                      bark tongue
                                            came cleft
                                    came claim

descent of long tail tits
makes whole the tree

       make whole of the tree
       in movement over

                                                    FP

```
                        limbs lay down to live
                more, longer


                    brittle below
          leafing above



    crack opened

           is its own eye

    scape on water


                              snapped through dead wood
                         sat on mossed bark (trunk?)
                      feet rest curve, head in
                 branch-placed
            within when
        song voices   many-silhouetted  spreading
    glade yellow-green up
                          flickering for midges
          from above
                     just when
          we weren't writing
                         and to next place     on
```

                                                                HT

Hey Clough
September 14

Crack willow (salix fragilis): stems break (crack) easily at branch points. Often found alongside rivers and flooding.

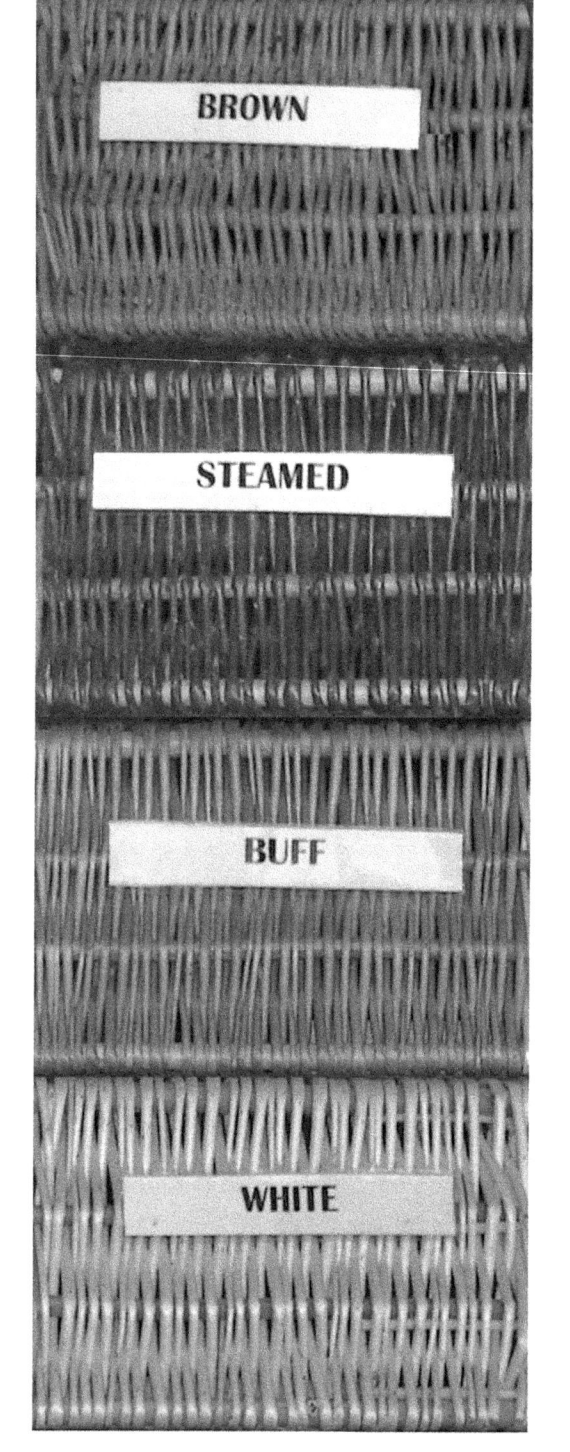

```
                        limbs lay down to live
              more, longer

                     brittle below
         leafing above


   crack opened

           is its own eye

    scape on water

                              snapped through dead wood
                         sat on mossed bark (trunk?)
                      feet rest curve, head in
                   branch-placed
              within when
       song voices   many-silhouetted  spreading
  glade yellow-green up
                         flickering for midges
        from above
                  just when
        we weren't writing
                         and to next place      on
```

                                                                HT

Hey Clough
September 14

Crack willow (salix fragilis): stems break (crack) easily at branch points. Often found alongside rivers and flooding.

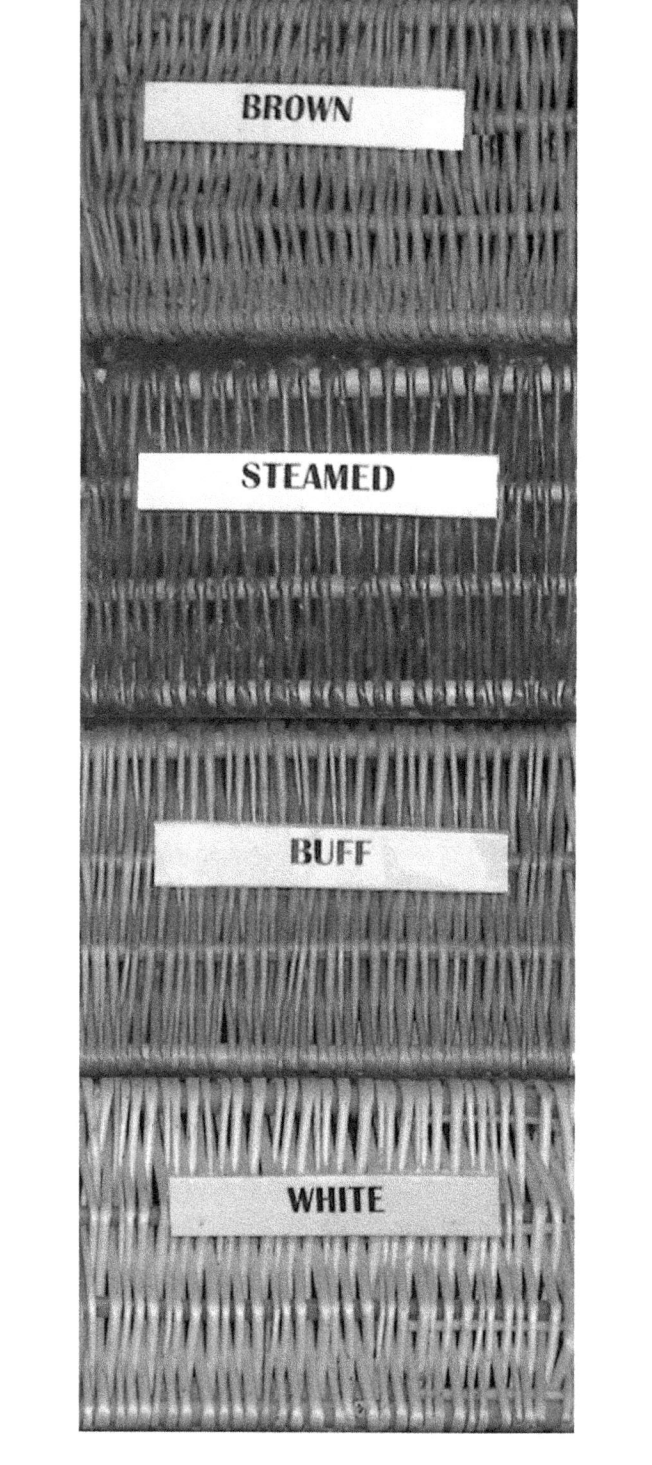

sallow

tear off a small shoot
so green
it will not tear
bite through with teeth

     sp / lits
into strips

       back of a green fur clad
          gremlin
              rears up
  pointed   pinned back
                        ears
shouldering up
    breaking down

    an   army   of   shoots
    block   ade

why break into it there?
it doesn't make sense
    without her voice

                here we live
                      on benefits
                            of   ~~*national trust*~~

                parkland can be entered for £5 a year

                  Griff Rhys Jones interviews a local tenant
                  her sallow teeth
                  tell the benefice
                            of an allotment

this benefice to water
a combe
where eyes adjust to shadow

```
        slew            slew            slew
            slu             slu             slu
sluice

    sel                         worthy
            se                      le
    soul                sale
        sa                  lee
            sa                      low
                sally
                                hoo
```

Selworthy combe
December 14

grey willow

      forge   Lafarge
      tarmac   put on
      the block   mega
      merger quick set
      to   post   crete

green leaves are bramble
blackbird calls   back off

   pressed down to the river
    slide down the leaning
                lichen bark
    fissured branches

   base of rust grey

          ( )

    oval leaves

                          sluggish the Yare
                         reflection to pylon
                      ice clear in the water

                              power lines
                              are ripples
                          willow shoots

Whitlingham
January 15

alder carr

    orange alder
    merges in water

    brown ink foliage
    made shape of tree

    ground of burnt sienna
        unfinished
      at time of death

        a small figure
            on the bank
                slides

into water

                into fire

John Sell Cotman
c. 1840-42

swamp carr

locked off   boardwalk
rotten planks   no   boat
permit   hold

uneven   depression
                            sedge   tussock   green
                       spears   circle
               thin   yellow   root   raft

alder   leans   across the river
                   too   far   to   reach

     dead   ivy   stem   on trunk   spinal   fossil   vertebrae
                  proceeds   by   exoskelet   exocet

    soft root mound   early nettles
       moss and bramble
            sinking me
     all the   way   into   marsh
                       methane

          roll myself   back to shore

light upper side   white lichen trunk
                leaning away   dark trunk
                        stretching across
                            from opposite bank

           alders   lock   branches

         r
    a   c

Ranworth Broad
March 15

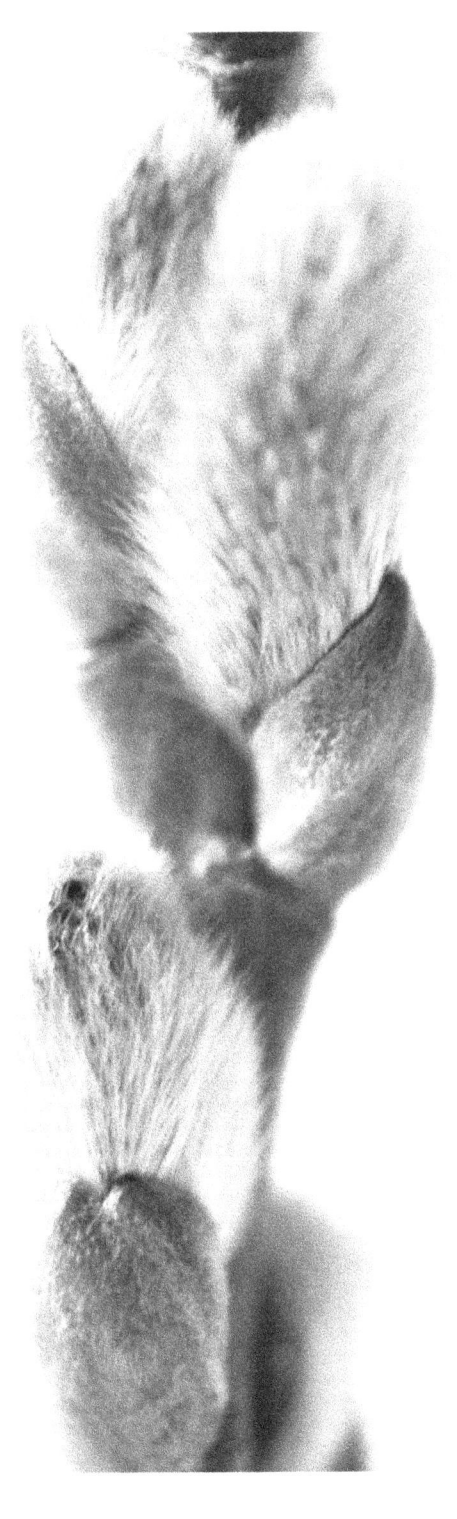

pussy willow

for Libby

blue sky   blue Liam Fox
billboards   uniform light
blue   broad brush   tree logo
secure union flag   to fit foliage

dead trunk   M5   cracked
  off   Gordano welcome
    breaks the gor   dam
founders   in mud valley

pussy willow
 reaches across the ditch
        over the   rhyn/me
plants its feet   on the other side

white floss   fluff
   cat's paws floating
       on dark shallow water
           deep bed of leaf mould

seed   scatterers
  white   smudges
   saffron   centipede
      surface   progress

we are dioecious
   male/ female catkins
          tips   point
tips receive   pollen

botanising girls
*   plant prostitutes*
* should stick to ferns &*
celebrate marriage in the dark

she has crossed the remnant bridge
           to black earth & flag iris

in a flicker of stills
     she lifts one foot
          out of the deep peat bog

throws down dead branches
        lifts the other foot
           and then the other

     lays a sweet track

Gordano valley
April 15

wysywyg

    narrow   green   leaf   tapers
                  under   water

              submerged branches

                  ramifications
                       in the Usk aquarium

no   Private Fishing

no dark surrounds
                or eyeliners

why worry about eye bags
                and mud packs

    density and insistence of bird song
      underline   emphasise

    lose my emphasis

        you are thinking
        why approach from this direction
        why put the tree before the driver

tadpoles cling to the mud bank
              rapid shelf
                    flicking tails
                          propel

    rise
   to feather
    branches

     rise
    to leaf
     rise
    to light

              shoals are wholes
                         and take direction

shift my eyes between willow leaf light
          and   sand still   half light below

                             shaded rooms

we are between two worlds

    given one last thing
                love
                    bre ath on eir ic
                          letters

river ~ afon   Usk ~ Wysg ~ fish

May 15

sallow

sallow continues a long sequence of poems about the languages of trees, halse for hazel (Shearsman, 2014). 'Halse' is Exmoor dialect for hazel, transcribed by local historian Hazel Eardley-Wilmot in an essay on place names which are derived from trees. This convergence of names initiated a new poetic syntax of marginal trees, women and languages. The personal significance of place names has interested me since I first read HD's Her: 'Pennsylvania. Names are in people, people are in names. Sylvania. I was born here... Trees are in people. People are in trees.'

sallow is both a species of willow and dull skin: its dual meaning is in the title poem, where 'sally' is dialect for sallow and a girl's name.

As well as local dialect, I use the languages of forestry and botany, analysing and reassembling them. I benefited from the guidance of botanist and poet Libby Houston.

halse for hazel began on the hills of Exmoor and in sallow I wanted to explore trees in low lying, wetland areas, such as willow and alder. The sequence maps political and environmental pressures, as well as recent catastrophic flooding: 'willow' was written on a train in the Somerset Levels when the surrounding fields were an inland sea.

Many of the poems were written on site which can be hazardous, as it was in swamp carr at Ranworth Broad, but the trees have their own agency, and need to be experienced close up, whether in the wild or the urban edgelands of 'grey willow'.

The reinvention of language and form is often shaped by the inventiveness of wild trees. sallow explores the visual patterns we use for trees in the design of the text and visual poetics. 'Crack willow' is from a walk with Harriet Tarlo near her home in Yorkshire. I sent her my text, she interleaved a response, and our two versions are printed on facing pages.

The Somerset poems were part of a collaborative performance with Robert Minhinnick which gave them a sharp linguistic and political focus.

sallow, like halse for hazel, has been a dialogue with the work of artist Irma Irsara.

Frances Presley
May 2016

www.ingramcontent.com/pod-product-compliance
Ingram Content Group UK Ltd.
Pitfield, Milton Keynes, MK11 3LW, UK
UKHW022217230426
12048UKWH00016BA/908